WORKING FOR SOCIAL JUSTICE

TAKING ACTION

AGAINST INEQUALITY

Rita Santos

Enslow Publishing
101 W. 23rd Street
Suite 240
New York, NY 10011
USA
enslow.com

Published in 2020 by Enslow Publishing, LLC.
101 W. 23rd Street, Suite 240, New York, NY 10011

Library of Congress Cataloging-in-Publication Data

Names: Santos, Rita, author.
Title: Taking action against inequality / Rita Santos.
Description: New York : Enslow Publishing, 2020 | Series: Working for
social justice | Audience: Grade level 3-6. | Includes bibliographical
references and index.
Identifiers: LCCN 2018050008| ISBN 9781978507883 (library bound) | ISBN
9781978508019 (pbk.) | ISBN 9781978508026 (6 pack)
Subjects: LCSH: Equality—Juvenile literature. | Economic policy—Juvenile
literature.
Classification: LCC HM821 .S176 2019 | DDC 305—dc23
LC record available at https://lccn.loc.gov/2018050008

Printed in the United States of America

To Our Readers: We have done our best to make sure all website addresses in this book were active and appropriate when we went to press. However, the author and the publisher have no control over and assume no liability for the material available on those websites or on any websites they may link to. Any comments or suggestions can be sent by email to customerservice@enslow.com.

Photo Credits: Cover, pp. 1, 19 © AP Images; p. 5 Rawpixel.com/Shutterstock.com; p. 6 J. Bicking/Shutterstock.com; p. 9 CaseyMartin/Shutterstock.com; p. 11 Robert Crum/Shutterstock.com; pp. 12, 25 Monkey Business Images/Shutterstock.com; p. 14 Iakov Filimonov/Shutterstock.com; p. 17 Wayhome studio/Shutterstock.com; p. 21 Marko Poplasen/Shutterstock.com; p. 22 wavebreakmedia/Shutterstock.com; p. 27 a katz/Shutterstock.com; p. 28 Valerie Macon/AFP/Getty Images; cover graphics Stankovic/Shutterstock.com.

CONTENTS

INTRODUCTION

We live in a **diverse** world. People belong to many different groups or communities based on things about them like their ethnicity or religion. Each of these groups forms a different part of their **identity**. Most communities strive to treat people with **equality**. This means that, no matter who you are, you have the same rights and opportunities as anyone else. But equality doesn't mean we all get the same things. For example, a person with poor eyesight needs glasses. Equality means making sure people with poor vision have glasses, not that everyone has glasses. Equality means we are all treated fairly.

Unfortunately, some people are still treated unfairly because of who they are. When people are treated badly because of some part of their identity, like their race or sexual orientation, it's called discrimination. When people are treated badly by their government, it's called **oppression**. People can be discriminated against for many reasons. Discrimination is always wrong, but it can be hard to stop.

Discrimination causes inequalities in our communities because it prevents everyone from getting what they need. When people are discriminated against, they can have trouble finding jobs. They may be charged more for things

We live in a diverse world, and we need to make sure that everyone is treated fairly.

Some groups, like LGBT people, have been discriminated against by the government because of who they are.

they need than other groups or have more trouble finding housing. Discrimination also makes our communities unsafe because it can create fear of and anger toward people based on their differences—and can lead to even more serious problems like violence against minorities.

Being a part of a community means we take care of each other. It means we are all on the same team. No matter what community we belong to, we all have a responsibility to make sure no one suffers from inequality. By learning to fight inequality we can make our communities even better. Inequality is unfair but it's not unstoppable. We can work together to end discrimination.

one

WHEN SOCIETY IS UNEQUAL

Every community has rules and systems that help it run. Think of these systems like the directions to a board game. Good directions make sure that every player starts the game with everything they need to play. But board games only work when everyone plays by the same rules. Some inequality in our communities is caused when people play by different societal rules.

We like to think that anyone who breaks a law will receive the same punishment. However, studies have shown that white people who are found guilty of crimes receive less punishment than people of color. This kind of racial inequality is bad for everyone. It means some people are punished too much and others not enough.

Like a board game, every community has rules that have to be followed to keep it running properly.

But inequality can start even earlier in a person's life. Some people are born with more advantages than others. This makes it easier for them to take care of themselves and pursue their life goals. A person with fewer advantages may need more help from society to achieve the same goals. Inequality means some people are not getting the things they need to live happy, healthy lives. No one deserves to suffer because their family has less money or because they are a minority.

WHERE DOES INEQUALITY COME FROM

It's easy to think that inequality is caused by the actions of a few terrible people. In reality, most people don't want to cause inequality to happen or continue. But whether we know it or not, we all take part in systems that are unequal.

In the United States, public schools are free and funded by local taxes. This means each family in a town pays some money to help the schools buy things like textbooks. This system seems fair because everyone can attend school for free. However, because some neighborhoods are wealthier than others,

Inherited Wealth

When parents can pass money or other things of value down to their children, it's called **inherited wealth**. Some groups were once prevented from owning homes. This meant they had less inherited wealth to pass along to their children. Those children likely had white peers who *were* able to benefit from inherited wealth since their parents weren't prevented from owning a house. This is an example of how inequality in the past can still affect families today. Understanding the effects of past discrimination can help us solve current problems with inequality.

When parents pass property, like a house, onto their children, this is called "inherited wealth."

Public schools are supported by local taxes, which means schools in wealthier neighborhoods are better funded.

schools aren't always funded equally, which is unfair to low-income students.

To battle inequality, we must understand how different people are affected by society's rules and systems. Sometimes things that seem fair aren't really fair for everyone. Learning how to spot inequality is a big job.

two

SPOTTING INEQUALITY

It can be helpful to think of inequality like an iceberg. An iceberg is a floating block of ice that can be large enough to sink a ship. It's hard to tell how large an iceberg is from above the waterline because only a small piece of the ice may be visible. Good sailors know how to spot possible icebergs and when they need a closer look. Inequality in our society can be the same way. Many issues around inequality can seem small until we take a closer look.

By taking an active interest in how people who are different from us experience the world we can begin to learn to spot some of their inequality icebergs.

Many women have experienced scary street harassment, with men they don't know approaching or shouting at them.

SMALL INEQUALITIES

Some forms of inequality, like segregation, are too big not to notice, but acts of inequality can sometimes be hard to spot if they aren't happening to you. We rarely notice the small ways other people may be treated differently than us when we go out in public. Many women have had the experience of walking somewhere and having a strange man yell something terrible at them. This is called street harassment. It usually happens when women are walking alone or when other men aren't around. It is a humiliating and scary experience for many women. Because it often happens when other men aren't around, men are less likely to notice it happening or how frequently it happens. They are unable to see how big the problem is.

These kinds of inequalities often need to be pointed out to people who don't experience them. Social media campaigns can be a powerful way to show just how common these small forms of inequality are. The hashtag #YesAllWomen was used by women to share their experiences with

Privilege

Everyone has certain advantages and disadvantages in life. Something that is beneficial in some situations can be a disadvantage in others. Being very tall can help you play basketball but it can make riding in cars less comfortable. When something is an advantage, we sometimes call it a privilege. We all have different kinds of privilege depending on the situation. Acknowledging your privilege means understanding the ways certain situations may be easier for you.

harassment, both from strangers and from friends, acquaintances, and even bosses. It helped start a national conversation about how women are treated.

LISTEN AND BELIEVE

It's important to believe people when they share experiences that are different from your own. They have firsthand knowledge that you may lack, the same way you may have knowledge of experiences that they lack. It's important to share our experiences with inequality so that we can all learn to treat each other better.

Social media hashtags have drawn attention to issues like sexual harassment.

One fun way to learn about the lives of other people is to read books and watch movies that are made by people from other cultures. Books are especially good at helping us understand how other people experience the world. Even a work of fiction can help you learn about the specific challenges faced by other communities.

three

SPEAKING UP

Bullying is a problem in many schools. If you've ever been bullied, you probably know that ignoring a bully doesn't make them stop. You probably had very little control over your bully's actions. But if your classmates decide not to play with the bully until they treat you better, that might be enough to make them stop.

Unfortunately, school isn't the only place with bullies. Some people think it's okay to treat people who are different from them badly. These people are **intolerant** of others. They often try to convince people who are like them that people who are different are bad.

SAYING NO TO FEAR

Some people are intolerant of immigrants. To convince others that immigrants are bad they may

While some people may fear them, immigrants have come to the United States to build a better life for themselves and their families.

talk about times when immigrants have committed crimes against citizens. They talk about immigrants as though they are all the same. Intolerant people know the threat of crime is very scary. They want to make you scared so that you will agree with them and support laws that keep immigrants out. In reality, immigrants are much less likely to commit crimes than citizens are.

Intolerant people want us to believe that inequality is okay in certain cases, but that is never true. They try to make people afraid of those who are different from them. When someone tries to use the actions of a few people to justify treating a whole group of people badly, they are being intolerant. Some people think the best way to deal with intolerant people is to ignore them. But intolerant people, like bullies, won't stop until their community tells them their views are unacceptable.

TALKING ABOUT INTOLERANCE

Standing up to a bully can be scary. People are afraid to speak out because they don't want to be bullied themselves. But when everyone stands together, the bully loses power. Speaking out against intolerance and inequality works the same way. When we hear other people say intolerant things, we have a responsibility to politely correct them.

Many intolerant people don't understand why their beliefs are wrong. When we hear someone say

Stereotypes

You've probably noticed that toys for boys tend to be blue or green while girls' toys tend to be pink or purple. These toys are promoting a stereotype that all boys and all girls like the same colors. But we all know girls who love blue or boys who love purple. Stereotypes want us to believe that people in certain groups are all the same. But no group of people is exactly alike. So while it's true that some girls love pink, the stereotype that *all* girls love pink is untrue.

Stereotypes might make us think that boys shouldn't play with dolls, but both boys and girls can play with whatever toys they want.

When you see a bully picking on someone, it may be hard to speak out, but it is important to stand up for other people.

something intolerant, it's best to explain why what they said was incorrect. When we correct others, it's important to focus on *why* what they said was wrong rather than who they are as a person. Saying something wrong doesn't mean we're bad people, it just means we need more information. When we take the time to explain intolerance, we can help change people's minds and make the world a more welcoming place for everyone. However, if an intolerant person threatens you or someone you know, tell an adult immediately.

four

TAKING ACTION

One of the best ways to fight inequality in our communities is to get to know our neighbors. When we learn what problems our friends have, we can try to help them. Different neighborhoods face different problems. Try to notice instances of inequality where you live. What problems are caused by inequality? See if there are any community groups you could volunteer with to help solve the problem. If homelessness is an issue where you live, you could help by volunteering to work in a soup kitchen.

BECOME AN ALLY

When we see our friends being bullied, we're more likely to stick up for them. But it's even more powerful to stand up for people even if they aren't our close friends. Sometimes the best thing we can do to fight intolerance and inequality is to become

Getting to know your neighbors is a great way to build a sense of community and learn how you can be of service.

an ally. An ally is someone who sticks up for the rights of communities or groups of people that they don't belong to, the same way you'd stand up to your friend's bully. Good allies listen to the problems of others without judgment. They help those in power learn about issues other communities are facing.

Social Media

Social media can be a great way to raise awareness of issues of inequality, but it can be harmful as well. Before you believe what you read online, make sure you do your research. Find out where the information is coming from. Do you trust the source? Does it make **generalizations** about people? Intolerant posts can be hard to spot. If your friend posts something intolerant, try talking to them in person about why their post was harmful. It's possible your friend was unaware of the post's hurtful aspects.

The Black Lives Matter movement was created to bring awareness to the number of black Americans who are killed by police officers every year. Many black Americans believe that they are discriminated against by police officers. Unfortunately, many people outside the black community were unaware of the violence being committed against their fellow citizens. By sharing stories of police violence against black citizens while using the hashtag #blacklivesmatter, people use social media to show that they have noticed the problem. Allies of all

The #BlackLivesMatter movement has helped people learn about the many black Americans killed by police officers every year.

races now use it to show their support for the black community. Sometimes the best thing we can do as allies is to share information about injustice against other communities with our own communities so that we can all recognize the problem and work on a solution together.

Marley Dias created change in her community by starting #1000blackgirlbooks, a book drive focused on getting more books with young black women as main characters into schools.

MAKING A DIFFERENCE

Fighting inequality is everyone's responsibility. You're never too young to start! In 2016, eleven-year-old Marley Dias became frustrated by the fact that none of the books in her classroom had characters like her, a young girl of color. She wanted more characters she could relate to. She started a book drive at her school called #1000blackgirlbooks. The campaign made national news. It drew attention to the need for more diverse books in schools. By speaking up about an inequality she experienced, Marley was able to help other children find books with characters that represented their own experiences and identities.

What can you do in your community to help take action against inequality?

Words to Know

discrimination The unfair treatment of people based on something they cannot control, like their race or sexual orientation.

diverse When things are different from each other.

equality The idea that everyone should have what they need to succeed.

generalization A belief that because some people of a certain group behave or feel a certain way, all people of that group behave or feel that way.

identity The core of who we are as people, made up of our likes and dislikes as well as the groups we belong to and ideas we believe in.

inherited wealth Money or other valuable things that children receive from their parents.

intolerant Disliking people from other communities.

oppression Unfair treatment of a group of people by a ruling government.

Learn More

Books

Manushkin, Fran. *Happy in Our Skin*. Somerville, MA: Candlewick, 2018.

McMeans, Julia. *Justice in Our Society* (Civic Values). New York, NY: Cavendish, 2018.

Mirza, Sandrine. *People of Peace: Meet 40 Amazing Activists*. London, UK: Wide Eyed Editions, 2018.

Websites

Kids Against Bullying

pacerkidsagainstbullying.org

This site inspires students to take action against bullying in their schools.

Race Project Kids

understandingrace.org/kids.html

Understand what it's like to walk in someone else's shoes at the Race Project.

Teaching Tolerance

splcenter.org/teaching-tolerance

Learn more about the fight to end discrimination.

INDEX